Science WHY?

WHY DOES JELLY WOBBLE?

Om KIDZ
An imprint of Om Books International

WHY?

CONTENTS

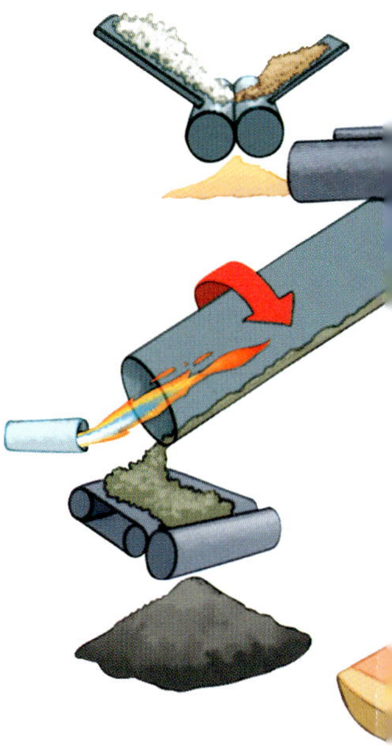

Find out!

Who was the first person to invent cement?

1 Why doesn't glue stick to the bottle it is in?

Because there's no air! Glue contains water and chemicals. When you apply glue on something you want to stick, water in the glue comes in contact with air and evaporates. This makes things stick together. But when glue is inside a bottle, the water in the glue does not get enough air to evaporate. This keeps the glue in its liquid state and doesn't get stuck to the bottle!

Pocket fact

Krazy glue was invented accidently by Harry Coover while attempting to make plastic lenses for rifle sights. It was impossible to work with this glue because it stuck to everything!

2 Why is cement strong enough to bind bricks?

It is a binder, like glue! Cement acts as an adhesive when it dries and holds bricks and stones together. It is made by heating clay and limestone in a big oven called a kiln. Heating brings changes in the metals, and converts to a hard substance called clinker. Clinker is powdered and mixed with gypsum, a soft white or grey coloured mineral. This makes cement ready for use!

Find out!

What is the speed of sound?

3 Why does a pencil look bent in a glass of water?

Because of refraction of light! Refraction is a change in direction of light when it travels through different mediums. Light travels in air, vacuum and water at different speeds. When light enters water, it cannot move as fast as it does in air. On entering water, refraction occurs. Light bends away from its path. This is why the pencil (or any object) immersed in a glass of water, appears bent.

Pocket fact

A lens uses refraction to form an image of an object for many different purposes. Interestingly, a prism uses refraction to form a spectrum of colours from an incident beam of light.

4 Why can't I hear anything in vacuum?

As vacuum does not have particles that can vibrate! Sound is a wave and is created when a movement causes vibrations in its surrounding particles (atoms or molecules). Atoms and molecules are found everywhere except in a vacuum. When sound vibrations reach the tiny hair in your ear drum, you hear sound. Since there are no molecules in vacuum, no vibrations occur. The sound doesn't travel, and you cannot hear anything.

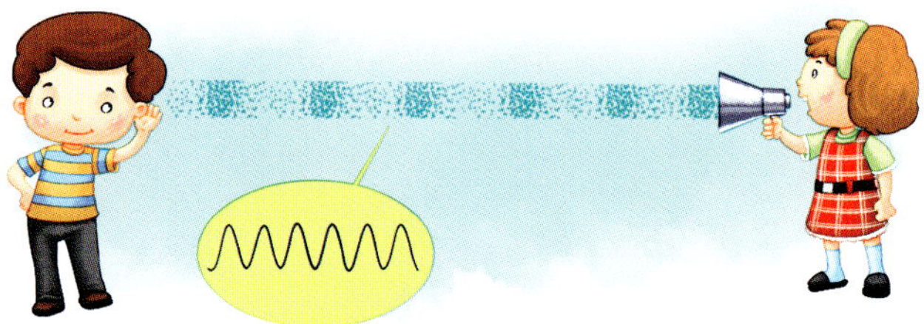

Find out!

Why does a golf ball have dimples?

5 Why is a tennis ball fuzzy?

To help the ball move at a balanced speed! A tennis ball is fuzzy because it allows the ball to move forward without increasing its speed too much. When the tennis ball strikes the racquet, it lightly grips the ball's fuzz and controls its movement. When the ball moves at slower speeds, the fuzz allows it to move faster and when the ball reaches a higher speed, the fuzz helps control the speed of the tennis ball.

Pocket fact

Tyres were white for the first 25 years after the invention of cars. This was because zinc oxide was added to the rubber in order to make them strong. This gave tyres the bright white colour.

6 Why are tyres black?

For their protection! Vehicle tyres are black because a chemical called carbon black is mixed in them during the manufacturing process. This increases the strength of the tyres and also protects them against the harmful ultra violet (UV) rays from the Sun. Sun's UV rays can wear out and crack the tyres. Carbon black converts the UV radiations into heat thus protecting the tyre.

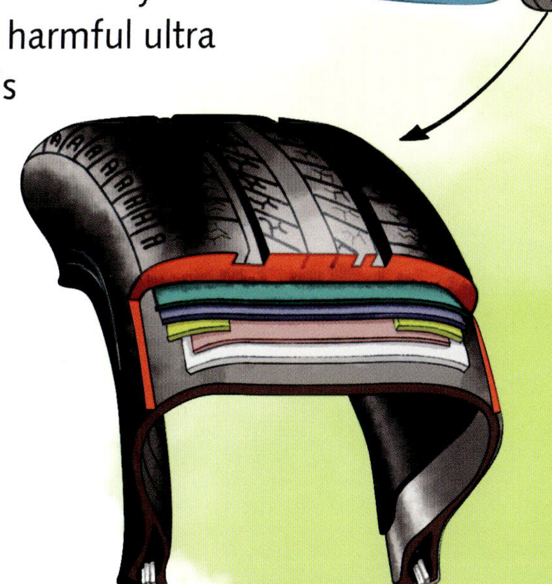

Find out!

Who made teflon first?

7 Why do some cooking utensils have wooden or plastic handles?

To protect you from getting burnt! Cooking utensils are made of metals that are good conductors of heat. If the handles are also made of metal, they will absorb heat. So, if you pick a utensil by the metal handle, it can burn you! On the other hand, wood and some durable plastics do not allow heat to pass through them. So handles made of wood or plastic make it easy for you to handle cooking utensils.

Pocket fact

The most widely used material for cookware (on gas stoves) are stainless steel, copper and aluminium. Stainless steel is made by adding chromium and nickel to steel. This makes it highly anti-corrosive.

8 Why doesn't food stick to non-stick pans?

As it has no friction at all! Non-stick pans have a coating of teflon. Teflon is known as polytetrafluoroethylene (PTFE), a compound of carbon and fluorine. The coating of teflon on non-stick pans makes the pans smooth and slippery. The smoothness of the surface offers no friction. The lack of friction doesn't allow food to get stuck on these pans.

Find out!

From which plant is menthol extracted?

9 Why does mint gum make my mouth feel cold?

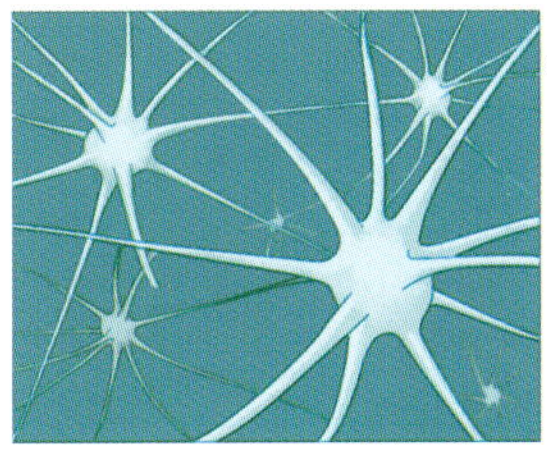

The secret is menthol! Mint gum contains menthol that binds with cold-sensitive receptors in your skin. These receptors have some channels called TRPM8. The menthol makes these receptors very sensitive and gives you a cold sensation. The sensation is colder if you drink water just after having a mint gum!

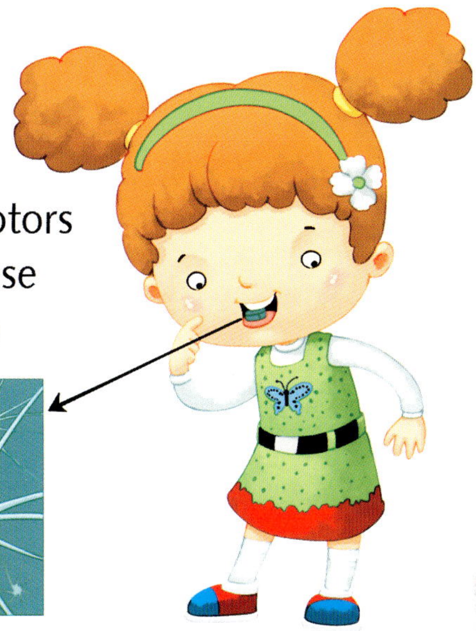

10 Why is chlorine added to swimming pool water?

Pocket fact

Chlorine is found in the most common substance we use in our food. It is in sodium chloride better known as 'common salt'.

To kill bacteria! The water in a swimming pool may be infected with bacteria as a lot of people use the pool. When we go for a swim, bacteria from our bodies escape into the pool. When chlorine gas (in its liquid form) is added directly to the water, a hypochlorite ion is formed. This ion releases oxygen. The released oxygen then reacts with all organic matter and kills the bacteria!

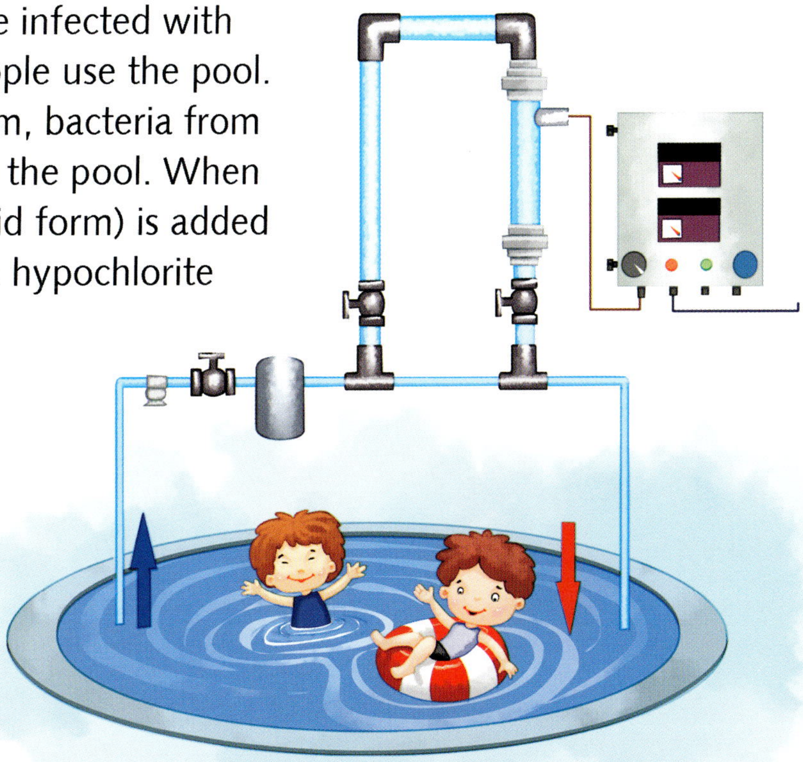

Find out!

Can you list names of any five things that do not dissolve in water?

11 Why is water colourless?

Because it absorbs all the colours of white light! White light is made of seven colours. When light falls on an object, it absorbs some colours and reflects others. The reflected colour reaches our eyes and the object appears to be of that colour. For example, when you look at mango juice, all colours from the light are absorbed, except yellow. Yellow colour reaches our eyes and, therefore, the juice looks yellow. When light falls on water, it reflects all colours, except a tiny tint of blue. This makes water appear transparent and colourless.

Pocket fact

It is interesting to know that hot water freezes faster than cold water. This is known as the Mpemba Effect. No one knows the secret behind it!

12 Why does adding salt to water make it freeze slowly?

Salt lowers the freezing point of water! Water changes to ice at a temperature of 0° Celsius. This temperature is called the freezing point of water. When you add salt to it, salt molecules occupy space between water molecules and the water molecules repel these salt molecules. This makes it harder for water molecules to bond with the ice structure; thus preventing water from freezing at 0° celsius.

Find out!

What do you call two liquids that do not mix with each other?

13 Why is butter usually yellow?

Carotene gives butter its colour! Butter has a natural pigment called carotene. Carotene is fat soluble; it is transferred to milk fat and then into the butter, giving it the yellow tint. The amount of carotene depends on a cow's feed. Cows feed mostly on hay, silage, grains and cereals, which produce carotene rich dairy. Sometimes, artificial pigments are also added to butter to enhance the yellow colour. When the amount of carotene is low, butter gets a natural white colour instead of yellow.

Pocket fact

Artificial colour has been added to butter since about 800 years! During the Middle Ages marigold flowers were used to enhance the yellow colour of the butter.

14 Why doesn't oil mix with water?

Both behave differently with each other! Water molecules have a small positive (+) charge at one end, and a small negative (-) charge at the other end, so they stick to each other. But oil molecules don't have any charge. This is why they are not attracted to water molecules but to each other. This prevents oil from mixing with water. In fact, oil floats on water because it is less dense than water.

15 Why do jet planes leave a trail of smoke behind?

Find out!

How many wheels does an aeroplane usually have?

Water and carbon dioxide form the trail! Jet planes fly 26,000 feet above the sea level. The air is very cold at such a great height. As a jet plane flies, hot water vapour and carbon dioxide is released from its engine, which come in contact with the freezing air outside. So, water vapour changes to water and ice particles immediately. These particles attract more water molecules towards them and the tiny drops of water form clouds. This leaves a trail called 'contrail' as the jet moves forward!

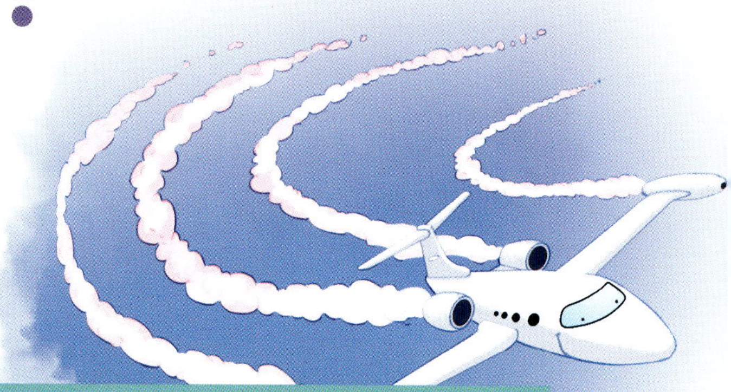

Pocket fact

The world's fastest manned jet airplane is the U.S. Air Force's SR-71 Blackbird. It flies at more than 3,220 kmph.

16 Why do aeroplanes need wheels?

To help them take off and land! The wheels of an aeroplane support it when it is not in air, allowing it to take off and land without damage. Aeroplanes need to move forward to maintain lift. The wheels reduce friction with the runway. This makes the aeroplane move more easily while taking off, and while landing the friction reduces the movement helping the plane to stop smoothly.

Find out!

What is naphthalene made from?

17 Why do moth balls keep moths away from clothes?

By emitting vapour! Moth balls are small balls made of either naphthalene or para dichlorobenzene. The chemicals, naphthalene and dichlorobenzene undergo sublimation, i.e, they evaporate from a solid state directly into a gaseous state. This gas is toxic to moth and its larvae and thus keeps moths away from our clothes!

Pocket fact

The first artificial sponges!
Artificial sponges were first developed by the Du Pont Company in the 1940s.

18 Why does sponge absorb so much water easily?

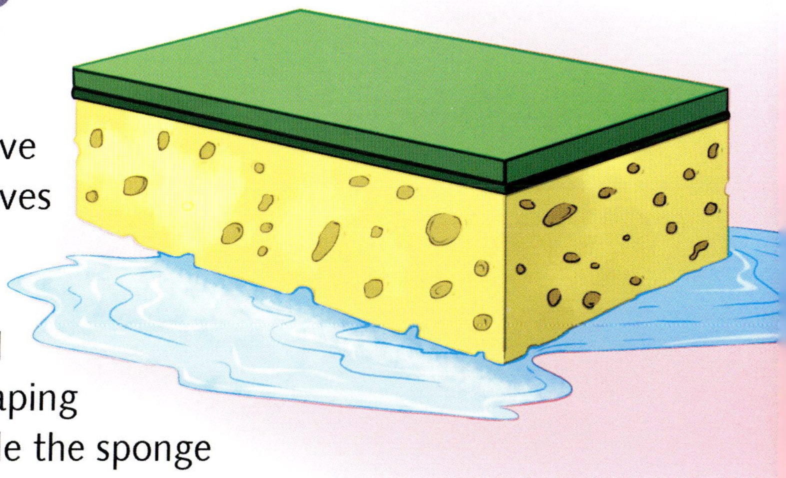

Loose fibres help it absorb water! A sponge is made of loose fibers that have empty space in it. This empty space gives sponge all its properties. The empty space between the fibers soak up water. This causes the fibrous material to swell and stops the water from escaping the sponge. The water is trapped inside the sponge until you squeeze it!

Find out!

When was the first commercial bubble gum made?

19 Why does jelly wobble?

Because it has gelatin! Jelly is made from gelatin and fruit flavours. When gelatin molecules are warmed in water they are long, but when cooled some of these get intertwined with others and form a bigger molecule, which also branches out like a tree. This process continues and forms new 'supermolecules' and form a 'net' stretched across the material. This net makes the jelly wobble.

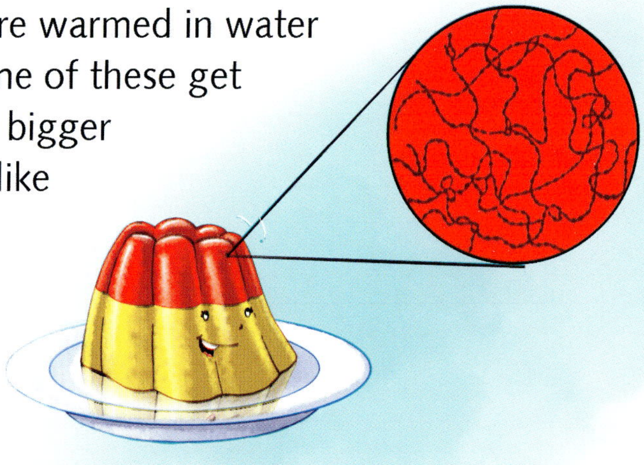

Pocket fact

In 1997, the British Army's Logistics Corp helped make the world's biggest jelly at the Blackpool Zoo. It was almost one metre tall and seven metre wide. It took about 12 hours to set the jelly using a blast chiller.

20 Why is chewing gum stretchy?

Chewing gum is made from the sap of the manilkara chicle tree. The sap is called chicle and is mainly used to make chewing gums. Chewing gums have long chains of tiny particles called atoms strung together. The strings are cross-linked and tangled with each other. This links one strand with another at several places and makes the chewing gum rubbery and stretchy.

Find out!

Who discovered chlorine as a bleaching agent?

21 Why does soap not make lather sometimes?

Only when hard water is used! Soap has natural fatty oils and chemicals like sodium hydroxide. When you use soap in water, a frothy white mass of bubbles is produced by it. This is called lather. Soap doesn't form lather when used in hard water. Hard water contains a lot of calcium and magnesium salts. These salts cause the soap to precipitate and it can't form lather.

Pocket fact

Besides humans, soaps are used for cleaning animals as well. Murphy's Oil Soap is a soap used especially to clean elephants!

22 Why does bleach make clothes white?

It releases oxygen! Chemical compounds called chromophores reflect a certain part of the visible spectrum of light and we see different colours. When bleach is applied on clothes, oxygen molecules are released in a process called oxidation. These oxygen molecules break up the chemical bonds of chromophores. The chromophores then reflect no colour thus making the clothes appear white.

Find out!

Name the shrub on which jumping beans grow.

23 Why do jumping beans jump?

Jumping beans are not beans but seed pods of a shrub that grows in Northern Mexico and Southwest America. These seed pods have the larva of a small grey moth inside them. The larva enters the seed pod and eats it, once the seed is eaten, the larva lives inside the empty pod. When you warm these beans the larva start wiggling and makes the beans jump!

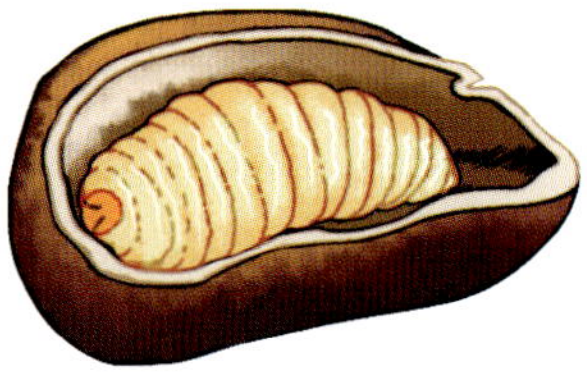

Pocket fact

You can tell if an egg is raw or hard-boiled by simply spinning it! A hard-boiled egg spins easily but a raw egg wobbles.

24 Why do some eggs crack while boiling?

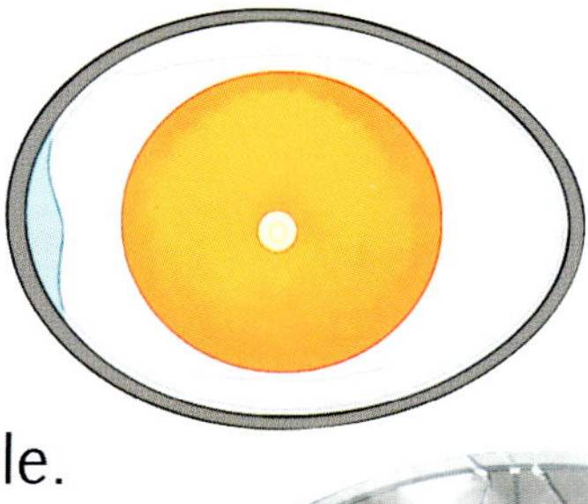

Because they have air inside! The bottom, rounded end of an egg has a small air bubble. When you boil an egg, it heats up and the air inside the bubble expands. The hot air now pushes outwards and puts pressure onto the shell. This makes the shell crack, as a result some eggs crack while boiling.

Find out!
Why do wires in electric appliances or switches have different colours?

25 Why are electric wires covered with plastic?

To prevent us from getting an electric shock! Electric wires are made of copper which is a good conductor of electricity. But these wires are coated with rubber or plastic because both plastic and rubber are bad conductors of electricity. So, when you touch the wire, you won't get an electric shock since plastic doesn't allow electricity to reach your body. Also, plastic is flexible and bends easily around corners and fits into electrical boxes safely.

26 Why do most ceiling fans have three blades?

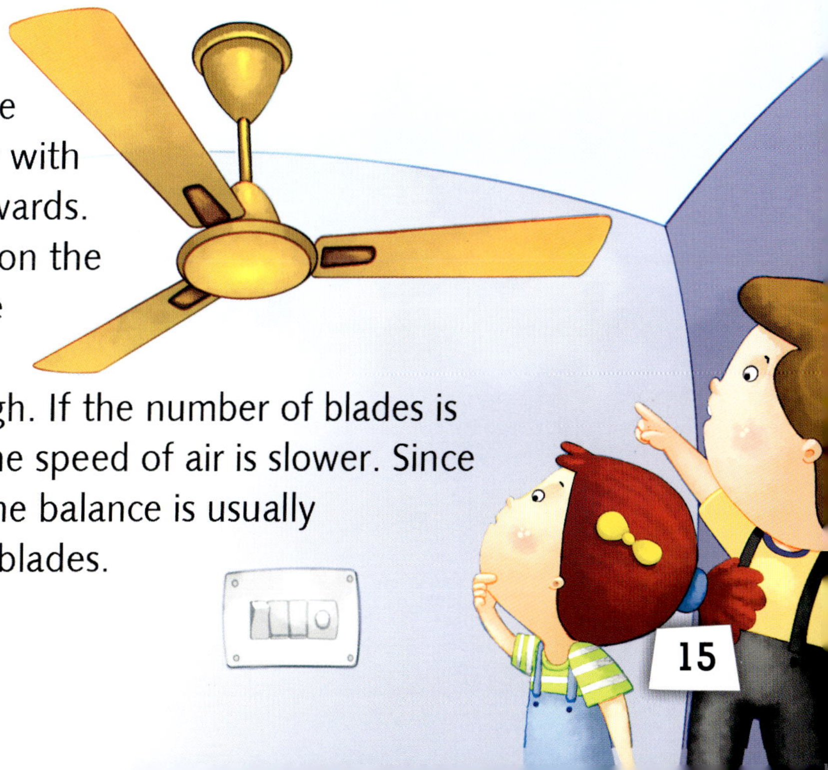

To push more air as it rotates! A ceiling fan circulates air, making us feel cool. The air circulates when the blades of the fan cut the path of air with its blades and pushes the air downwards. The air pushed by the fan depends on the number of blades it has. If there are more blades, the volume of the air to push is less but speed of air is high. If the number of blades is less the volume of air is more but the speed of air is slower. Since a fan cannot have just one blade, the balance is usually maintained by having two or three blades.

OTHER TITLES IN THIS SERIES